LAWRENCE E. SULLIVAN

THE COSMOS AND WISDOM OF
TAOISM

CHELSEA HOUSE PUBLISHERS
PHILADELPHIA

CONTENTS

A silk tapestry of the Eight Immortals, men who in Daoist tradition obtained immortality by following different paths; they are not the only Immortals, but they are the emblems of the varied human conditions. Here they are celebrating a long life, the result of a life well lived, while a new Immortal ascends to Heaven on a crane, the symbol of purity. Daoism, which gathered various Chinese traditions on the art of living for a long time, appears as the title-holder of the secret knowledge of vitality. The concept of Daoist immortality depends on the ability of man to return to the breast of that primordial Oneness that is eternal. The road of return has various levels through which a person may, at a minimum, attain longevity.

RELIGIONS OF HUMANITY

RELIGIONS OF HUMANITY

Chelsea House Publishers
1974 Sproul Road, Suite 400
Broomall, PA 19008

The Chelsea House
world wide web address is
www.chelseahouse.com

English-language edition
© 2002 by Chelsea House
Publishers, a subsidiary
of Haights Cross
Communications
All rights reserved.

First Printing

1 3 5 7 9 6 4 2

Library of Congress Cataloging-in-Publication
Data Applied For:
ISBN: 0-7910-6647-9

© 2001 by
Editoriale Jaca Book spa, Milan
All rights reserved.
Originally published by
Editoriale Jaca Book, Milan, Italy

Design
Jaca Book

Original English text by
Lawrence E. Sullivan

*Right: In Changling, a prayer and an
offering of incense sticks are among the
most common Daoist devotions.
Located northwest of Beijing,
Changling is one of the thirteen
necropolises of the Ming dynasty.
Selecting the best site and space follows
the ancient art of geomancy, or "feng
shui," which translates as water and
wind, and signifies the knowledge of
building in favorable locations in
favorable ways. In fact, the
arrangement of space is of the greatest
importance in Daoism. The study of the
flow of water and air, in their
relationship to hills, light and shadow,
determines the concentration of
favorable cosmic influences, allowing
the avoidance of those that
are harmful.*

*Facing page: One of the thousands of
canals in Suzhou. A city of waters and
gardens, wrapped by the Grand Canal
which connects the delta of the Huang
He, or Yellow River, to Beijing, it is
furrowed by a thick interweaving of
canals. Water for Daoism is the symbol
of the cohesion and the unity of the
Elements and of adaptability and
fluidity. The canal is a daily presence
in the life of the inhabitants.*

INTRODUCTION

Daoism (also spelled Taoism—see glossary) is an important feature of religious life in China today, just as it has been for thousands of years. Daoism cultivates wisdom and physical well being, including longevity and even physical immortality. In the Daoist view, the human being is an image of the universe. Energies that drive the universe, which is the active cosmic body, also empower the human body, which is active in religious ritual, physical discipline, and in mental exercise. Daoism offers practices for the body and understandings for the mind. Together these practices and ideas provide access to the *Dao*, the supreme source of all reality. Breathing, movement, healing, and nutrition are physical exercises that preserve and increase vital energy. Meditation, interior hygiene, and philosophy are mental exercises that produce effective visions of renewal. Daoism nourishes itself on contrasts, starting with its intention to foster wholeness without striving for it. Over centuries, Daoism has generated folk festivals for community celebrations and has compiled Scriptures and developed philosophies for individual study. Daoism integrates routine practices into everyday life, and, at the same time, produces mystical and magical techniques linked to extraordinary religious experiences. By mastering numerous spirits and identifying gods by name, Daoist leaders have established separate movements within Daoism. After achieving immortality, these leaders transmitted their rites and teachings to their followers. An official collection of Daoist texts, the *Tao Tsang*, was published in 1926 in Shanghai. The *Tao Tsang* was collected in 1436 C.E. in 1,120 volumes, but an earlier collection of these texts, burned by Kublai Khan in 1281 C.E., was even longer. The rich and complex tradition of Daoism is outlined in the following chapters.

In China, interest in astronomy dates back many centuries as was noted by European visitors like Matteo Ricci, who shared the passion for the exact observation of the stars. Even the most technical Chinese disciplines which focus on human beings place them in a vision of the cosmos, intended as the sole, animated reality, always in motion; a manifestation of an ultimate reality that Daoists and Confucians call Dao. Like each aspect of ancient Chinese science, the observation of the heavenly bodies is inscribed in a cosmology. In the photograph: an historical observatory in Beijing.

1
DIVIDING THE NEW FIRE: "FEN-DENG"

1. *A sign of devotion and prayer in a Daoist temple in Hong Kong.*

2. *A Daoist priest. Ministers of this cult can be people who dedicate themselves solely to it, residents of the temple or monastery compounds, and even lay people assigned to domestic rites.*

In the brief meditation called *fa-lu*, the Daoist high priest purifies the hearts and minds of the devotees. The meditation empties them of images and spirits which crowd inside, in order to make space for the *Dao*. New fire is lit by striking sparks from fresh flint: the first ceremonial candle of the Daoist religious rites is set aflame to renew the cosmos. Then the new fire is carefully divided in a rite called *Fen-Deng*. The first candle brings to light the visible *Dao* known as *Taiji*, the power of primordial breath associated with the highest level of the natural world and linked to the realm of thought. The first candle also stands for *San jing*, the ancient spirit who governs heaven. Next, the fire of *Taiji* is used to light a second candle whose flame makes visible the soul that lives within the loving human heart. This second candle represents *Lingbao*, the spirit who rules the earth, the central level of the cosmos. Finally, fire is passed to a third candle associated with the watery underworld of the cosmos as well as the human mid-section, with its gut instincts and intuitions. The third candle stands for the spirit *Daode*, who rules water and rebirth. The *Fen-Deng*, though a simple set of gestures, reenacts the emergence of the world from the *Dao*, a process described in the forty-second chapter of the *Dao de jing*:

> "The Way bears one.
> The one bears two.
> The two bear three.
> The three bear the ten thousand things.
> The ten thousand things
> carry the *yin* on their shoulders
> and hold in their arms the *yang*,
> whose interplay of energy
> makes harmony."

(from *Lao Tzu, Tao Teh Ching* by Ursula K. LeGuin. © 1997 by Ursula K. LeGuin. Reprinted by arrangement with Shambhala Publications, Inc., Boston, www.shambhala.com).

Through the *Fen-Deng*, and its ritual actions, human beings participate in the powerful relationships that emerge from the *Dao* on every level of existence.

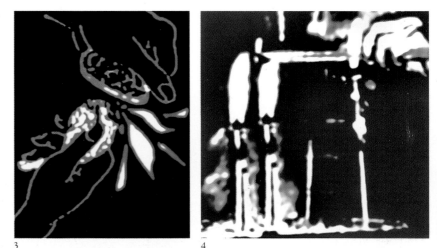

3. *Striking flint in order to attain sparks and fire is a technique which has been used from prehistoric times to today.*
4. *On the altars of Daoist temples candles are always lit; a gesture that assumes a special importance during rituals like the one of the new fire.*
5. *Sunset on the Yellow River. Its waters allowed the first Chinese agriculture and were symbolic of life and rebirth for many generations.*

2
RENEWAL AND UNION: PLANTING AND EATING THE ELEMENTS

1. A graphic representation of a bas-relief tile found in an ancient tomb from Sichuan province; a scene of the rice harvest attests to its centuries-old importance.

Two important rituals oppose one another like bookends. The first rite is often called *Suqi*; and it is performed during the first day of the *Jiao* renewal festival. During the *Suqi*, the five basic elements are planted. The second ritual of the opposing pair is called *Daojang* or *Cheng-jiao*, performed during the last day of the renewal festival, when the five elements are harvested and eaten. Around the time of the winter solstice, for example, these two rites are used to open and close the *Jiao* festival of renewal. During the opening *Suqi* the ritual leader sets five bushels of rice in an order that outlines the whole world: a bushel set in the East, another in the South, West, North, and Center of the 'world.' In each bushel he then plants a basic element: wood, fire, metal, water, and earth respectively. These 'elements' are composed of magical signs drawn on five colored silk cloths: green, red, white, black, and yellow respectively. Standing in the 'center of the world,' the Daoist ritual master makes an arrangement with the spiritual forces of the universe to obtain a good seed-time, growing season, and rich harvest along with health and happiness for all.

The *Daojang* (or *Cheng-jiao*) ritual, held on the final day of

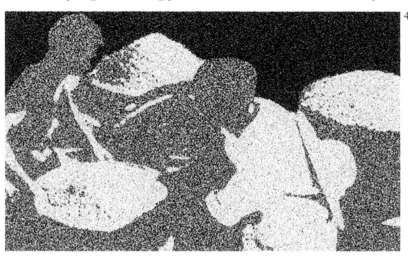

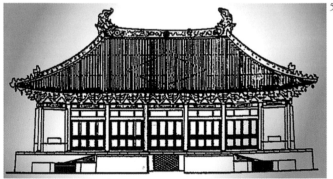

2. The drawing shows a small portion of the grand system of irrigation which China has used for centuries. From its origins, the control of the waters has been a vital problem to which many mythical tales are tied.
3. Today rice cultivation shapes and colors the south of China (province of Sichuan).
4. The drawing shows the transportation of piles of rice, a daily operation which a ritual can transform, giving it symbolic value.
5. In the drawing: the Temple of the Three Pure Ones (Shanxi Province). The Three Pure Ones are the personification of Dao. Their power is especially honored in various forms for the celebration of the Jiao festival.

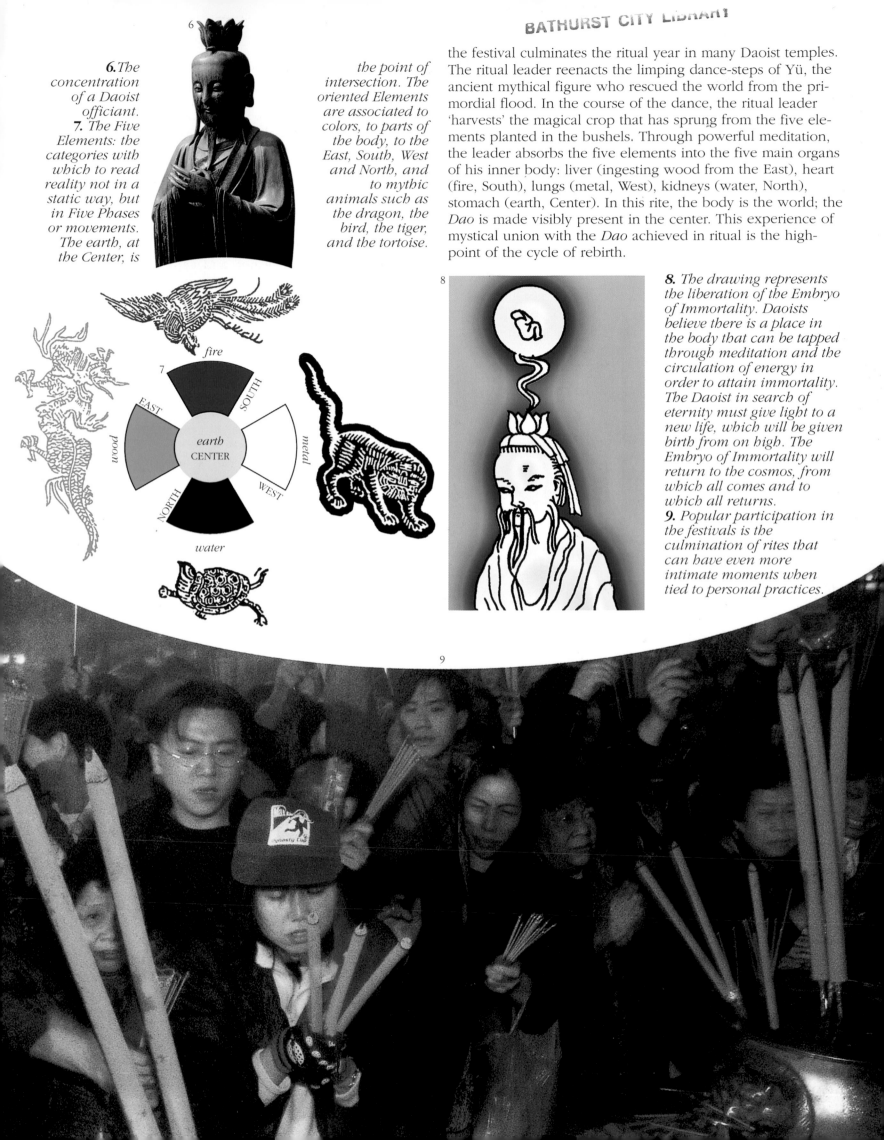

6. The concentration of a Daoist officiant.
7. The Five Elements: the categories with which to read reality not in a static way, but in Five Phases or movements. The earth, at the Center, is the point of intersection. The oriented Elements are associated to colors, to parts of the body, to the East, South, West and North, and to mythic animals such as the dragon, the bird, the tiger, and the tortoise.

the festival culminates the ritual year in many Daoist temples. The ritual leader reenacts the limping dance-steps of Yü, the ancient mythical figure who rescued the world from the primordial flood. In the course of the dance, the ritual leader 'harvests' the magical crop that has sprung from the five elements planted in the bushels. Through powerful meditation, the leader absorbs the five elements into the five main organs of his inner body: liver (ingesting wood from the East), heart (fire, South), lungs (metal, West), kidneys (water, North), stomach (earth, Center). In this rite, the body is the world; the *Dao* is made visibly present in the center. This experience of mystical union with the *Dao* achieved in ritual is the highpoint of the cycle of rebirth.

8. The drawing represents the liberation of the Embryo of Immortality. Daoists believe there is a place in the body that can be tapped through meditation and the circulation of energy in order to attain immortality. The Daoist in search of eternity must give light to a new life, which will be given birth from on high. The Embryo of Immortality will return to the cosmos, from which all comes and to which all returns.
9. Popular participation in the festivals is the culmination of rites that can have even more intimate moments when tied to personal practices.

3

CHANGE THROUGH TIME

Various forms of Daoist practice and thought appear throughout its long history. Already in the beginning of the Imperial Era (221 B.C.E..-220 C.E.) systematic writing on Daoist ideas such as *taiping*, "great peace," described this ideal of perfect harmony among all of the world's realities. The *Tianshi* (Heavenly Master) tradition, which promised to achieve the "great peace" based itself on the thought of Zhang Dao-ling in the second century and that of his grandson in the third century. Over the centuries, Chinese rulers depended on Daoist leaders who communicated directly with Lao-jun, a deity identified with Lao-zi, who was credited with writing the *Dao de jing*. The Heavenly Master tradition changed from the fourth century onward in ongoing contact with southern China. One

transformation, for example, was called *Shangqing* Daoism and it based its changes on revealing visions received from *shenren*, divine beings or immortals living on mythical mountains. *Shenren* had the power to appear, disappear, and multiply, changing at will by perfecting the techniques of alchemy and visualization. They dwelled on the Isles of the Blessed in Kun-lun, the heavenly mountain that one climbed along the path of self-perfection. From these mystical vantage points, the *shenren* enter *Dongtian*, the holy caves that provide access to the inner womb of the earth where the immeasurable treasures of health and revealed wisdom are hidden. From the fourth century onward *Lingbao* Daoism fostered public liturgies that linked individuals with nature and with society on a

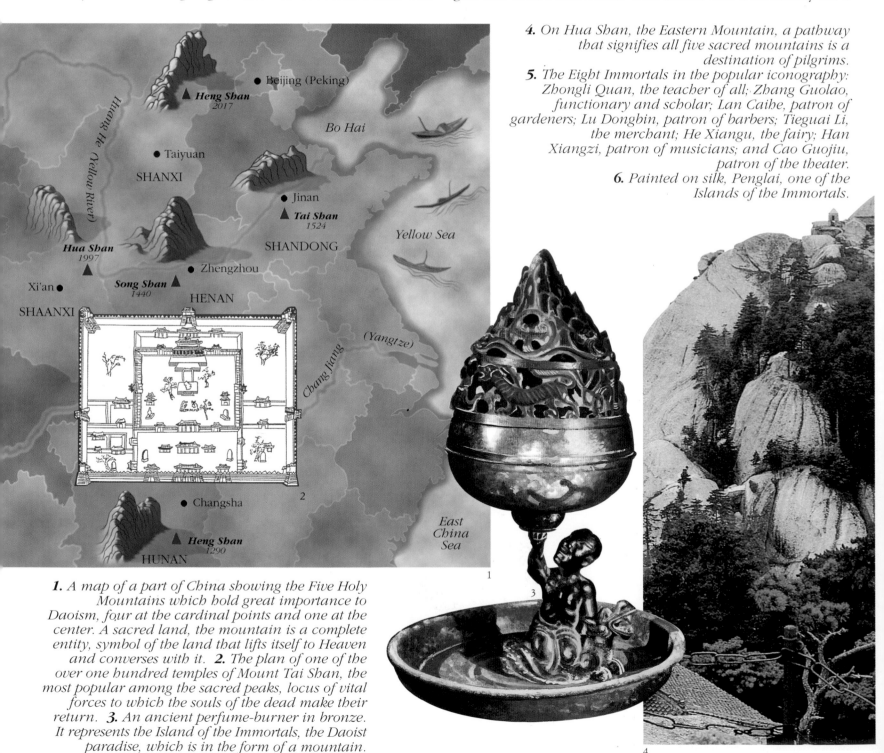

4. On Hua Shan, the Eastern Mountain, a pathway that signifies all five sacred mountains is a destination of pilgrims.
5. The Eight Immortals in the popular iconography: Zhongli Quan, the teacher of all; Zhang Guolao, functionary and scholar; Lan Caihe, patron of gardeners; Lu Dongbin, patron of barbers; Tieguai Li, the merchant; He Xiangu, the fairy; Han Xiangzi, patron of musicians; and Cao Guojiu, patron of the theater.
6. Painted on silk, Penglai, one of the Islands of the Immortals.

1. A map of a part of China showing the Five Holy Mountains which hold great importance to Daoism, four at the cardinal points and one at the center. A sacred land, the mountain is a complete entity, symbol of the land that lifts itself to Heaven and converses with it. 2. The plan of one of the over one hundred temples of Mount Tai Shan, the most popular among the sacred peaks, locus of vital forces to which the souls of the dead make their return. 3. An ancient perfume-burner in bronze. It represents the Island of the Immortals, the Daoist paradise, which is in the form of a mountain.

common path toward salvation. Mongol rule that began in the twelfth century, as well as in the Ming and Qing dynasties, suppressed Daoist groups as well as other religious organizations. During this period of repression, a separate mystical form of Daoism emerged which stressed the importance of individual meditation. Daoist liturgical and mystical practices continue today, even though Daoism was outlawed in the People's Republic of China for a period during the mid-twentieth century.

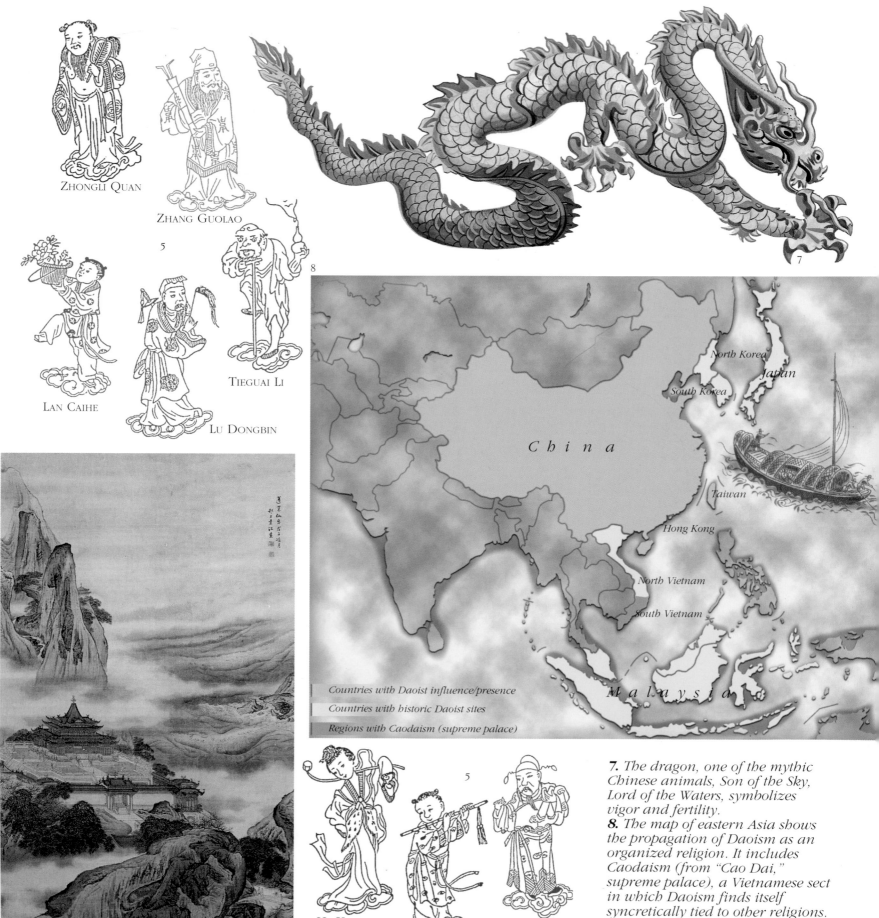

ZHONGLI QUAN

ZHANG GUOLAO

5

LAN CAIHE

LU DONGBIN

TIEGUAI LI

8

China

North Korea

South Korea

Japan

Taiwan

Hong Kong

North Vietnam

South Vietnam

Malaysia

Countries with Daoist influence/presence

Countries with historic Daoist sites

Regions with Caodaism (supreme palace)

HE XIANGU

HAN XIANGZI

CAO GUOJIU

5

7. *The dragon, one of the mythic Chinese animals, Son of the Sky, Lord of the Waters, symbolizes vigor and fertility.*
8. *The map of eastern Asia shows the propagation of Daoism as an organized religion. It includes Caodaism (from "Cao Dai," supreme palace), a Vietnamese sect in which Daoism finds itself syncretically tied to other religions.*

6

7

13

4
"DAO"

The Chinese word *dao* means "way" in several senses of the word: a road or path, a way of life, a discipline or method to follow closely. In Daoist religious thought, *dao* means a teaching, doctrine, rule of conduct, or valuable speech. The idea runs in two different directions at the same time. On the one hand, *dao* is a power that transcends any reality, including the human mind: *dao* is inconceivable and unnameable. As the mystery of all mysteries, it remains impossible to describe, incomprehensible. On the other hand, *dao* is the ground of reality; the inexhaustibly fertile womb where all reality runs through its cycle of conception, gestation, and birth and to which all realities return in their cycles of death and rebirth. Thus *dao* is both a force beyond any single expression in nature and, at the same time, the force that flows within tangible nature, propelling it to change. *Dao* therefore embraces reality at its widest reach, both inward to the smallest speck of material existence and outward beyond all material expression. Natural reality is a ceaseless cycle spinning outward from the *dao* to all creatures, and cycling back to the *dao* for renewal, in keeping with the turning of the seasons in nature. Attuned

1. In this detail of a painting on paper, the artist, also known as "the hermit of the five peaks," represents a Daoist master meditating on a rocky promontory that extends over the valley, a symbolic representation of Emptiness, a hollow that gives birth to and nourishes everything and where vital breaths circulate freely.

2. Landscape of the Hua Shan mountains, on the waters of the Zuojiang river, in the province of Guangxi. The Chinese symbol for landscape is "mountain-water": the mountain as the microcosm of the great everything, water as fluidity, symbol of the way of Dao.

䷀	SKY
	THUNDER
	WATER
	MOUNTAIN
	EARTH
	WIND
	FIRE
	HAZE

太上老君說常清靜經
仙人葛玄曰吾得真道當誦此經萬遍是天人所習不傳
下士吾昔受之於東華帝君東華帝君受之於金闕帝君
金闕帝君受之於西王母皆口口相傳不記文字吾今於世書
而錄之上士悟之昇為天官中士悟之南宮列仙下士悟之在
世長年遊行三界昇入金門
左玄真人曰學道之士持誦此經萬遍十天善神衛護其
人玉符保身金液鍊形形神俱妙與道合真
正一真人曰家有此經悟解之者災障不生眾聖護門神
昇上界朝拜高尊功滿德就想感帝君誦持不退身騰

紫雲

水精宮道人書

to nature, human beings unite eternally with the *dao*. The way of the *dao* is especially evident in water: its flow, vitality, irresistibility, clarity, effortlessness, and shape-shifting conformation to the terrain. Water adapts to the sky, the earth, and the underworld, taking on distinct forms in each of these realms. Rulers and wizards who bring such diverse planes into fruitful contact are said to possess the power of the *dao* and bring human beings into communication with powers in heaven and on earth. Throughout Chinese history, kings manifest the power of *dao* by performing rituals that ward off disaster and renew nature through contact with the heavenly *dao*.

3. *I Ching, the classic Book of Changes is a divinatory text. According to an explainable cosmic law, change is the fabric of life. The possibilities of change are visualized with figures composed of complete and broken lines (yin and yang; see Chapter 6). In the drawing we see the basic aspects of change: the eight trigrams, when combined, form 64 hexagrams. By randomly selecting sticks or coins, cosmic changes, forces at play, and tendencies can be analyzed.*

4. *Detail of a roll of silk on which a sutra (from the Sanskrit for thread, rule) is written. It is the Daoist Sutra of Constant Purity and Tranquillity, that had been transmitted orally beginning with Lao-zi (see Chapter 5). It teaches that with the detachment of passions one will have a clear mind and a peaceful heart. Similar texts were transcribed in order to meditate on their contents. In fact, in China writing was born as a sacred activity.*

5
LAO-ZI

Lao-zi, the great and wise sage, holds a special place in Daoist thought and practice, where he plays several different roles. He is described as the author of the fundamental text of Daoism; he is also seen as a cosmic power and a divine figure. Already by the first century B.C.E., Lao-zi was regarded as the author of the *Dao de jing*, the principle book of Daoism and known also as *The Lao-zi*. Some ancient writings link Lao-zi to Lao Dan, "Old Man Tan" from whom Confucius apparently sought advice and instruction. The *Zhuang-zi*, written around 320 B.C.E. and attributed to an author of the same name, describes Lao Dan as an archivist from the Court of Zhou (1111-255 B.C.E.). This identification of Lao-zi with Lao Dan was developed in the first full-length biography of Lao-zi written by Sima Qian (145-86 B.C.E.), who tells the story of Lao-zi leaving the Zhou kingdom around the time of its downfall. Disillusioned by the realm's inability to cultivate goodness, Lao-zi moves westward through the Han-gu Pass towards Tibet. At the Han-gu Pass, a gatekeeper named Yin Xi asked Lao-zi to write down his ideas about *dao* and de. In three days, Laozi wrote the *Dao de jing* ("The Way and the Power of the Way"), a work written in five thousand characters on two scrolls. Scholars think that various authors contributed, right up until the last part of the third century B.C.E., to the text as it is known today. The *Dao de jing* ("The Way and the Power of the Way") remains the basic book of Daoist thinking. Moreover, the ideal teacher-student relationship is based on the model relationship that existed between the archivist-teacher Lao-zi and his gatekeeper-disciple Yin Xi, who met by chance in the high mountain pass thousands of years ago. By 165-167 C.E., the Emperor Huan allowed sacrifices to be offered to Lao-zi, who by then was revered as a primordial being, as ancient as the chaos that existed before the world emerged. After undergoing significant transformations, the ancient Lao-zi descended to the human realm to serve as sage counsel to the wisest kings of China. For centuries it was debated whether Lao-zi had also transformed himself into the Buddha after his westward journey in

5. *Dazu, in southern China, is known for the thousands of statues in its caves. Here the figures, appropriately Buddhist, are alternated with Daoist figures and Confucian themes, a joint presence of religious expressions, which appear to be arguing over the heart of the faithful.*

1. *Lao-zi, in his best known representation, is riding a buffalo.*
2. 3. *Portrait of Confucius, and from a relief on a tomb, his legendary meeting with Lao-zi. Anchored in the most ancient of traditions Daoism and Confucianism are the two great currents of Chinese thought.*
4. *From an etching reworked graphically, Lao-zi and the guardian of the West, his first follower.*

6. *Lao-zi is represented in a popular print as the Supreme One. In his hand he holds the diagram of the cosmos with the eight trigrams and the symbol of yin and yang. Four peaches, symbols of immortality, as well as stylized writing representing "long life," decorate his robes. At his side are two disciples, one holds a palm frond fan with magic powers, the other holds a copy of the "Dao de jing."*

order to bring barbarians knowledge of the "Way of the *Dao*." In one way or another, then, Lao-zi came to be seen as a savior and deity, the very source of the *Dao* from the beginning, who moved between the worlds of heaven and earth. In troubled times, his followers awaited his return to rescue them from oppression. The events of history were explained by using Lao-zi's absences and reincarnations to write about periods of prosperity and depravation. Lao-zi became a microcosm of the larger universe, embodying the *Dao* and serving as the mother of all things, the origin of all creation. Lao-zi encouraged the confession of sins and other forms of ritual purification as means of moral and physical cure. Taking Lao-zi as their example, Daoist meditators pictured themselves as the universe and, in their contemplative visions, journeyed throughout their inner landscape to quicken life forces on every plane. In this way, Daoist meditation focuses the disciple on the *zhen-shen*, the "true body" of Lao-zi, and on the landmarks changed by his passing. Similarly, the ritual actions of the Daoist priest during the *Jiao* renewal ceremony regenerate the embryo of the Lord Lao-zi inside the participating devotees and thus bring the entire community to salvation.

6

7

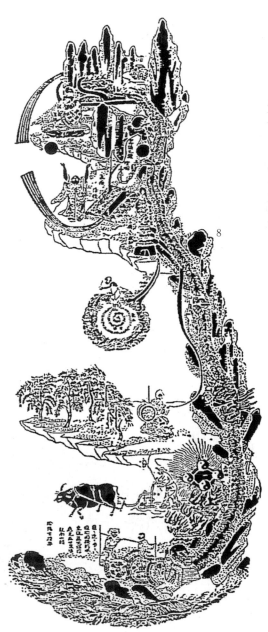

8

7. *A Zen garden near the Boston Museum of Fine Arts. Here the gravel represents water, and together with the rocks, symbols of the mountains, the garden appears as a landscape-symbol, expressing an image of nature inspired by Daoism. Daoism, which influenced Zen Buddhist Japanese monasteries, is also capable of influencing the West with the synthetic force of its meditative potential.*

8. *The drawing copies the Daoist representation of the body, seen as a landscape. The human being, rooted in the cosmic relationship Heaven/Earth, is also, on a smaller scale, a union of Heaven/Earth: organized, modeled, and maintained at the crossing of the constructive influences of Heaven and the docile and accepting ones of Earth, he is a knot of vital exchanges. This concept gave birth to the practice of traditional Chinese medicine which we have come to know as acupuncture.*

OPPOSITIONS AND PHASES:
"YIN/YANG"
AND "WU XING"

1. 2. *Two parts of a Japanese screen inspired by the great Chinese representations of the tiger and the dragon. Their symbolic strength is on a par: the two animals are often found together in Chinese tradition even in most ancient times. Opposite and complementary, their images have been found in tombs and have been interpreted as protective of clans and leaders. The dragon, son of Heaven and the divine emanation of the waterways, has always been integrated in the system of the yin and the yang; the tiger, a symbol of perfect energy, is the royal power of the animal kingdom, a concentration of vitality and effective virtues, whose vigor is often hidden by an apparent carelessness.*

Yin and *yang* are basic aspects of the *Dao*, as are the *Wu Xing*, the Five Elements or Five Phases. These terms are used to classify the relationships and realities that compose the world as Daoists see it.

Like the shady and sunny slopes of the same mountain, *yin* and *yang* are complementary opposites of the same reality. Sometimes symbolized as a dragon and a tiger, *yin* and *yang* are locked in a never-ending cosmic struggle that accounts for the dynamic developments of the visible world. The space of the world and the space of the body can be mapped in terms of *yin* and *yang*. The underworld of fire and water, associated with the belly in the human body, is a region of pure *yin*, divided into nine numbered sections, each one ruled by a destructive leader. The numbers are arranged in a magic square. At death, the souls move toward the *yin* realm where they are purified. Religious practitioners and spirit mediums contact the souls there and give voice to the desires that were never satisfied in life. The uppermost realm of heaven, associated with the head in the human body, is pure *yang*. Dead souls journey toward heaven when properly cleansed in the underworld and ritually assisted by the living. The earth sits in the middle level, corresponding to the chest in the human body; here *yin* and *yang* mix together and overlap. In this central realm Daoists carry out rituals that enliven the world and advance souls along their path by paying the required tolls to gatekeepers who control the path to their destiny.

The *Wu Xing* or Five Phases bear the names of the five basic material elements, each also possessing a number: (1) water, (2) fire, (3) wood, (4) metal, and (5) earth. These named elements are the basic influences that shape the world. Their names are the categories used to classify all kinds of relationships and realities: foods, directions, seasons, animals, colors, body parts, tastes, social activities, and so on. These categories organize philosophical thinking as well as such practical matters as eating a balanced diet harmonized with the seasons and the healthy functioning of the body.

3. 4. *In Mawangdui (Hunan), in the tomb of a lady from the 2nd century B.C.E., a cloth of painted silk testifies to a vision of the world and the importance of burials for the ancient Chinese. In the drawing, on the top: Heaven, with its spirits that move the world; at the center (and detail on the left): the rites for the deceased, with a bat holding Heaven; at the bottom: an atlas holding Earth.*
5. *Two laws on the dynamics of the Five Elements. On the left: wood generates fire, fire generates earth, earth generates metal, metal generates water, and water generates wood. On the right: to prevent imbalances, each Element is dominated and dominates. Wood dominates earth, deriving nourishment; fire dominates metal, melting it; earth dominates water, absorbing it; metal dominates wood, cutting it; water dominates fire, extinguishing it.*

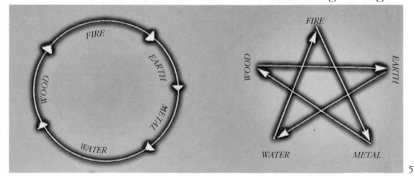

"QI" AND "WU WEI": VITAL ENERGY AND PURE EFFECT

Qi can mean "moist breath" or "vapor," referring to the vital energy that enlivens all beings in the cosmos. *Qi* is a central concern in Daoist religion and philosophy. Managing *Qi* so that it is aligned with and fed by the forces of the universe is the major aim of the techniques of self-control cultivated in Daoist meditation, ritual, diet, gymnastics, medicine, and philosophy. *Qi*, as a power of the *Dao*, streams throughout the cosmos and throughout the individual. Unhealthy habits and moral faults reduce the flow of *Qi*. But rigorous training of mind and body clear the channels and open the sluice-gates for the flow of *Qi*. Daoist practices maximize the flow of vital-izing energy, evident in philosophical wisdom and in physical health. Long life and even physical immortality can be the ultimate outcomes of the cultivation of *Qi*. *Qi* streams unimpeded when the individual is in a state of *Wu Wei*, a condition of creative quiet, as when a pool of water lies clear and still. *Wu Wei* consists of two opposed conditions that coexist at the same time: supreme relaxation and supreme creativity. *Wu Wei* is the condition of pure effect, an effectiveness never disrupted by striving. Human beings achieve *Wu Wei* only because they are open to the *Dao*, for *Wu Wei* cannot be created by human thought. Instead, it arises when the deeper unconscious

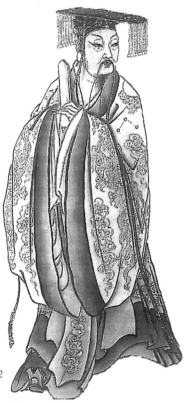

米
GRAINS OF
RICE

气
VAPOR

"QI"

1. Flowing waves, one of the exercises of the Straight Stick form, is one of the ways to train the vital breath which animates the universe and humankind.
2. Huangdi, the legendary Yellow Emperor, hero, civilizer, and great establisher of medicine, is a model of the art of living in Daoist harmony.

3. *Ideogram for Qi: by taking it apart we see the symbols for a grain of rice and for rising vapor. That which enables the rice to blossom and the vapor to rise is energy, the breath.*
4. *In Beijing, rising from an incense burner towards Heaven are spirals of vapor, the most immaterial aspect of energy, of which matter is one of the most condensed forms.*

mind contacts the life that is lived beyond the tension between separate forms and beyond the distraction of separate intentions. Like water that settles into cracks and crevices, *Wu Wei* appears effortless. It wastes no energy on process or display; no energy is spent on anything other than effect.

5. *In Hangzhou (Zhejiang province), jutting from the sparkling water of the Western Lake is a rocky formation, two emblems of nature with which human beings, as the crossroad of Heaven and Earth, are called to be in harmony.*
6. *In Monza (near Milano, Italy) students practice the initial phase of the "snake creeps down" form in a simplified style of Taiji quan, a "sweet" and ancient Chinese martial art. This simplification was created in China to be spread throughout the world. Taiji quan means Supreme Polarity of Movement and is a wide-ranging discipline where the Supreme Polarity, the wheel of existence, moves in a balanced way through the mutual transformations of Yin and Yang. The varying densities of energy in the different bodily zones are deliberately fostered and cared for.*

6

8
LIFE-CYCLE RITES

The power of the *Dao* manifests itself in the cycles of growth and renewal marked by the sun and moon, the gestation and growth of plants and animals, and in the procession of the seasons. Above all, Daoists mark the time of human life and the annual life of the cosmos by celebrating rituals at the major punctuation points. The human life-cycle has five phases, corresponding to *Wu Xing*, the five elemental phases: birth, growth, marriage, old age, and death. At each phase, special rituals are performed. Death rituals, for instance, can be very elaborate. They begin at the moment of death when white paper is set over the body and, at the same time, actions are performed near the ancestral shrine in the home. During the funeral, money offerings are made and incense is provided to assist the spirit of the deceased on its journey through the tollbooths and roadblocks of the underworld. Relatives enact scenes of the ideal burial, sometimes performing as many as twenty-four episodes that demonstrate the devotion children should have for honored parents. A model house is made of paper, including furniture and fixtures. A willow branch symbolizing the soul of the dead relative is brought back from the cemetery and installed on the family altar in the home. On the seventh, ninth, and forty-ninth days after the burial, additional ceremonies are held (as they may be also on the first and third anniversaries of death). The Daoist priest may accompany the deceased soul on a dramatic journey through the underworld, escorting it through the various gates of hell and conducting it past the demonic gatekeepers. At the proper moment, the paper house and other decorations are set afire.

1. Surrounded by the Eight Hexagrams, the Taiji symbol hangs over a tiger, the emblem of energy. The tiger has one black eye and one red eye, representing the manifestation of the yin and yang. It is an image of the vital movement that accompanies the human being along the course of existence.

4. *The Hall of Prayer for Good Harvest at the Temple of Heaven in Beijing where the Emperor would ask Heaven, which unfolds its activities in keeping with the rhythm of the seasons, for an abundant harvest. Any form of life is life under Heaven. The Chinese, not only Daoists, render homage to Heaven as the great regulator of beings. Heaven provides momentum and vigor for the universe.*

5. *A funeral procession from an early 20th century Chinese print. After a long walk accompanied by loud musical instruments, the procession will reach the Temple, the place for burial and rites.*

6. *A willow branch will be the reminder of the deceased within the home.*

2. *The scene of an ancient funeral which includes a decorated sarcophagus, ritual vases, and rows of bells played by expert musicians.*

3. *Constant in modern funerals are the models of earthly possessions. Here we see a house made out of paper.*

RITUAL RHYTHMS OF THE YEAR: THE CALENDAR

The yearly cycle of ceremonies swings back and forth between the odd, festival months marked by *yang* and the even, working months of agricultural labor marked by *yin*. Farm work and festivals alternate with one another because the festivals fortify the laborers and strengthen the growing crops. Some calendrical festivals stand out as more notable than others. The most important festival is the lunar New Year festival that takes place on the first day of the first month. In the most auspicious way, it ushers in the New Year and the forces of renewal. Families unite in special meals honoring their ancestors and their living elders. Special foods, with names and meanings particular to the occasion, are prepared in memory of the dead: special offerings are made at the family altar. The Festi-

val of Light (first month, fifteenth day) marks the first full moon of the New Year with processions of lanterns and floats as well as special dances and poetry recitals. The Lustration Festival (third month, third day) responds to the powers evident in the bright days of spring by offering sacrifices, special foods, and the cleaning of graves. These activities continue until one hundred and five days after the winter solstice. Summer Opening Day rituals (fifth month, fifth day) protect against sickness and maintain the health of children by performing ritual exorcisms and invigorations. Seven Sisters Day (seventh month, seventh day) celebrates the eternal courtship of the mythical spinning girl and her beloved cowherd boy. On the fifteenth day of the seventh month, Daoists hold a pre-

1. The lunar New Year is the Chinese festival which marks the end of winter and the rebirth of life. According to the remarks of the noted scholar Mircea Eliade, it acts as an aide to time so it may renew itself. The lunar calendar to which this celebration refers is in rhythm with the work in the fields and is followed to determine traditional festivals. In the photograph, the great colorful dragon, built for the festival and animated by men, careens through the streets of Hong Kong.
2. The New Year celebrations end with the Festival of Lanterns, a celebration of the victory of light over the darkness of winter. In the photograph: after the festivities are over, the lights in the lanterns are put out.
3. The incense spirals hanging from the temple ceilings are never extinguished during the festivities of the New Year, which they welcome with their intense aroma.

1   2

4. *The festivities are gladdened by eating and drinking with family and friends. Specific foods are associated with one or another celebration. In the photograph, special food is being served during a banquet in Korea.*

harvest festival at which all the souls of the dead are honored. For the duration of the festival rites, the deceased souls are freed from hell to attend the festive ceremonies. Special foods are set before them, just as the living enjoy their banquet. The Autumn Moon Festival is a harvest festival and thanksgiving feast held on the fifteenth day of the eight month. Round mooncakes are the hallmark food of the occasion, which is also marked by the recitation of poetry. Various winter festivals are held from the ninth month, ninth day until the eleventh month, eleventh day. This is the time when one is most likely to find celebrations of the *Jiao* renewal festival.

3

4

5

5. *Every phenomenon occurs between Heaven and Earth, whether intangible, like a sound, or solid, like cloth. Two mythic persons personify these qualities. Above all is the heavenly cowherd who tends the herds of Heaven and plays the flute. From its open holes, notes sound on the air. This is the way life is under Heaven. Humans also have analogous cavities which can sound to produce harmony. There is also the weaver, seated in Heaven in front of the cowherd, where she weaves and crosses her threads. Each of them synchronizes his movements to those of Heaven and Earth. In the drawing, a woman is concentrating at an ancient pedal loom.*

25

In the photograph: a suggestive vision of a bamboo forest. The image effectively expresses that which bamboo represents for the Chinese: the vital energy thrusting from Earth toward Heaven, with a dynamism considered the purest manifestation of the vegetal world and the incarnation of the Earth/Heaven dialogue from which all life takes form. Its great resistance, its flexibility, the adaptability of its wood to multiple uses, the ever green color of its fronds, have made bamboo the emblem of the virtues required of humans. Bamboo is the subject of innumerable paintings in China, Japan, Vietnam, and Korea, so much so that it is said that only a true painter knows how to paint it. The artist should depict the spirit of bamboo, which should throw its roots into the heart of humankind.

"MINDFUL OF LITTLE THINGS": *DAO DE JING*

From *Lao Tzu, Tao Teh Ching* by Ursula K. LeGuin. © 1997 by Ursula K. LeGuin. Reprinted by arrangement with Shambhala Publications, Inc., Boston, www.shambhala.com

六十四章

其安易持其未兆易謀其脆易泮其微易散為之於未有治之於未亂合抱之木生於毫末九層之臺起於累土千里之行始於足下為者敗之執者失之是以聖人無為故無敗無執故無失民之從事常於幾成而敗之慎終如始則無敗事是以聖人欲不欲不貴難得之貨學不學復眾人之所過以輔萬物之自然而不敢為

Chapter 64

It's easy to keep hold of what hasn't stirred,
easy to plan what hasn't occurred.
It's easy to shatter delicate things,
easy to scatter little things.
Do things before they happen.
Get them straight before they get mixed up.

The tree you can't reach your arms around
grew from a tiny seedling.
The nine-story tower rises
from a heap of clay.
The ten-thousand-mile journey
begins beneath your foot.

Do, and do wrong:
hold on, and lose.
Not doing, the wise soul
doesn't do it wrong,
and not holding on,
doesn't lose it.
(In all their undertakings,
it's just as they're almost finished
that people go wrong.
Mind the end as the beginning,
then it won't go wrong).

That's why the wise
want not to want,
care nothing for hard-won treasures,
learn not to be learned,
turn back to what people overlooked.
They go along with things as they are,
but don't presume to act.

GLOSSARY

The Chinese words are written in *pinyin*, the official system of spelling used in the People's Republic of China and used throughout the world. Alternate spellings, long known in English usage for common terms, are provided in parantheses, including the word Tao (for Dao), from which derive words such as Taoism and Taoist.

Dao (Tao) Literally means "way" in the strict sense of "road" but also in the figurative sense of "method," "doctrine," and "rule of conduct." *Dao* refers also to the power, both magical and religious, that kings and magicians use to make Heaven, Earth and humans communicate with one another. From the philosophical point of view, *Dao* underlies the order of nature, the order of the cosmos; but the word *Dao* also designates a specific philosophy, since each philosophical school has its *Dao*. In the outlook of religious Daoism, *Dao* is the ultimate reality that lies beyond all appearances and concepts.

Dao de jing **(Tao te ching)** Title of the work known as "The Way and the Power of the Way" (*jing* or *ching* means "book"), written in 5,000 characters on two scrolls. This is the fundamental text of Daoism. It consists of 81 chapters in the form of parallel verses and short poems, whose meanings are sometimes difficult to puzzle out, frequently based on oppositions. One of the essential notions is that of "non-striving" (*Wu Wei*, see below). Authorship of the *Dao de jing* is traditionally attributed to Lao-zi, even though scholars see the hands of several writers at work on the text from the 4th to the 3rd centuries B.C.E. The *Dao de jing* is used widely in various schools of Daoism, Confucianism, Chinese legalism, and Chinese folk practice.

Dongtian "Heavenly grottoes." Holy places in the form of mythical mountain caves, connected to one another via underground passages, where heaven becomes present and accessible. *Dongtian* are the womb of the earth, where the principles of life and holy scripture are kept hidden. The caverns are illuminated from within by their own light or by light rays that descend from heaven through special passages.

Fa-lu A brief meditation aimed at purifying the hearts and minds of the devotees by emptying all irrelevant images and disturbing thoughts.

Fen-Deng A Daoist ritual during which one lights three candles, each one with special significance. See chapter one.

Festival of Light Celebrates the first full moon of the New Year with a procession of lanterns, floats, dances and poems.

Jiao Festival A renewal festival, generally celebrated around the time of the winter solstice (see chapter 2).

Lao-zi (Lao-tzu) A sage living in the 5th century B.C.E., during a period called the epoch of the Warring Kingdoms. His name would have been Li, the archivist in the Zhou court, who left home because of the moral decadence of that kingdom. Tradition attributes to him the *Dao de jing* (The Book of the Way),

the fundamental book of Daoism. Legend has it that Lao-zi was born at the age of twenty-four, after having passed all that time meditating in his mother's womb. He is said to have died at 160 or 200 years of age, in keeping with the meaning of his name Lao-zi ("Old One"). Under the name Loazhun, Daoism reveres him as a divine figure.

Lingbao "Sacred treasure." A group of Daoist writings dating to the 4th century C.E. These texts focus on public liturgical practices performed on behalf of the living and the dead. The Daoism of *Lingbao* links individual spirituality to community practices (contrast with the Daoism of *Shangqing*).

Lunar New Year Festival It is a celebration of the New Year in the most auspicious way with certain rituals and customary practices signifying the meaning of renewal.

Lustration Festival *Qing-Ming*. Beginning the third day of the third lunar month, the festivities culminate on the 105th day after the winter solstice (April 4 or 5), thus joining the lunar calendar to the solar cycle. The Lustration Festival—also called the Spring Festival or the Pure and Bright Festival—is a prolonged purifying rite of spring, which links the life of the living to the commemoration of the dead and the ancestors: their tombs are cleaned; offerings are made; ancestral villages are visited.

Qi (Ch'*i*) "Moist breath." *Qi* is the energy, the vital force, that animates all creatures. The concept of breath gives rise to the meaning "vital spirit" or "vital power." *Qi* fills all forms of reality and the differences among them is due to the different conditions of *qi* (such as density, transparency, fluidity) and the different ways that *qi* is shaped into patterns by *li*, the basic ordering principles of existence.

Shangqing "High Purity." Group of Daoist texts from the 4th century C.E., issued by a sect that favored trance-states in their religious experience. Texts "revealed" in trances were set down through automatic writing and were considered as dictated to the mediums by the immortals or gods. Spiritual exercises consist of reciting these sacred texts and visualizing the scenes and spirits depicted in them. The Daoism of *Shangqing* is a way of meditation and personal spiritual realization (to compare and contrast with the Daoism of *Lingbao).*

Taiji The Great Ultimate Principle which lies at the origin of all created things and unites the cosmic forces of *yin* and *yang. Taiji* also expresses the essence of virtue and perfection.

Taiping "Great Peace" or "Great Purity." A doctrine expressed especially in the *Taipingjing* (Book of Great Peace)